DISAPPEARANCES

DISAPPEARANCES

KATHLEEN BELL

Shoestring Press

All rights reserved. No part of this work covered by the copyright herein may be reproduced or used in any means – graphic, electronic, or mechanical, including copying, recording, taping, or information storage and retrieval systems – without written permission of the publisher.

Printed by imprintdigital
Upton Pyne, Exeter
www.digital.imprint.co.uk

Typesetting and cover design by The Book Typesetters
us@thebooktypesetters.com
07422 598 168
www.thebooktypesetters.com

Published by Shoestring Press
19 Devonshire Avenue, Beeston, Nottingham, NG9 1BS
(0115) 925 1827
www.shoestringpress.co.uk

First published 2021
© Copyright: Kathleen Bell

The moral right of the author has been asserted.

ISBN 978-1-912524-76-1

ACKNOWLEDGEMENTS

Some poems have been previously published in the following journals and magazines: *Brittle Star, Hearing Voices, Litter, New Walk, Never (the Nottingham Writers Studio Journal), Poetry Nottingham, PN Review, The Coffee House, unarmed*; by Poem Flyer and Door-to-Everywhere; on the website of Nottingham Poetry Society; and in the anthologies *A Speaking Silence* (Indigo Dreams, 2013) and *Words in Concert* (Fort Worth Poetry Society, 2019).

Thanks are due to more people than I can list here. They include my children, Ellen Fife and Gerrard Bell-Fife; John Lucas for his editorial advice; Rachael and Nat Ravenlock of The Book Typesetters for their skills and patience; Ross Bradshaw and Pippa Hennessy and all the staff at Five Leaves Bookshop; and my former students and colleagues at De Montfort University, especially Simon Perril, Maria Taylor and Gina Greaves.

for David, with love

CONTENTS

BALANCE SHEETS FOR MEDIAEVAL SPINSTERS

the child	3
words from a homily	4
the lending	5
avoidance of sin	6
the long harvest	7
loss	8
longing	9
villein	10
hymn for St. Ursula, to be sung on her day	11
béguinage	12
anchoress	13
prayers requested of an anchoress	14
the wanton	15
la dame à la licorne	17
epitaph for an unknown princess	18
enclosure	19
Variations on a Half-Remembered Theme	22
After the Valley Was Flooded	24
Gelynos	25
At Alnwick Castle – after the wreck of the Forfarshire	26
Grace Poole, 1847	28
Malvolio in Prison	29
at the Chateau d'If	30
Driving to the moon, with ghosts	32
At Coldrum Stones	34
After Vermeer	35
Delft, 1661	36
David in Florence	37
After a self-portrait by Murillo	38
Palais des Beaux Arts	39
ad majorem Dei gloriam	40
Occupation	42

Painting in the Midi, 1942	43
at the vél' d'hiv'	44
The Fate Motif	45
Barbarians, AD 98	46
Watching Birds in Time of War	48
Testament: in an Embankment Garden	49

THE LITTLE BOOK OF ILLUSIONS: SCENES FROM A HISTORY OF MAGIC

transformation	53
the vanishing princess	55
instructions from Robert-Houdin	56
Robert-Houdin en Algérie	58
the aetherial suspension	59
sharper	61
restoration	64
unsundered	66
the private burying ground of Black Herman	68
Bess, 1936	72
at the station of Montparnasse	74

Balance Sheets for Mediaeval Spinsters

THE CHILD

The child you never had
was not pressed for the war
nor gone more years than you could count
on the fingers of one hand
while you hoped for word, never knowing
if he lived or cried for you at night
being, at thirteen years, not quite a man.

You never waited
for the child you never had
nor feared
for lice, damp, fever or the bad humours
that rise from earth in winter, drawing men
out of the air toward Hell's mouth.

Hell never cried out for this child
who was not born.
He was not prenticed to a bad master,
nor ever married to the village slut,
never betrayed nor scolded,
did not debauch himself into an early grave.

You never lay awake by rushlight, yearned to know
that he was well, that all was well with him.
Your eyes were never dry for lack of sleep
in long nights hunched over his sweat-soaked bed
or bent over the cradle he never used.

WORDS FROM A HOMILY

When the dead clamber out of their graves on that last day, you who are wife to no man will render your reckoning. Husbandless, you must stand surety for yourself.

When you are weighed in the balance, don't be found wanting. Your smallest transgressions will be stacked by Satan.

Silken pride will be measured against you and idleness, like lead, weigh down the scales.

You will weep for every fast you have broken. Your desires will cry out against you.

Did you steal? Did you scold? You deserve worse than death.

Pay for your sins now or wait for a worse purgation. Beseech or buy God's pardon while you can. The devils lurk, even at church-gate. They are eager to snatch you down.

Look to your life while you breathe or see your breathless body broken before you. Number your sins. Be watchful of all your ways.

Thank Christ for his kindness. Your earthly lord protects you: praise him.

For the Man of Mercy returns as Jesus the Judge.

THE LENDING

When I've performed my life
and come by Peter's Gate
to the great feast, then
You will look to Your lending.

Then You will say, "My child,
those two-score years I gave you
were no more than a loan.
The time has come to repay"

and I will reckon up
the little wealth I have:
the brief alms to a beggar,
the loyalty due my lord.

I followed fast and feast-days
according to Your season.
Keeping a fast was easy
for meat and fish were scarce.

Harder to sing Your praises,
harder to love my neighbour.
I knelt down in contrition
and paid You in my penance.

They say You value virgins
so this return I render:
a tree that bore no fruit
and a meadow left untilled.

AVOIDANCE OF SIN

Though marriage is ordained and godly
it is easy to fall into bad ways
such as gossip, scolding, unruly
desires of the will
or failure to bear a husband a living son.

Better to live chaste
though, in repayment,
nights may be lonely.
Some days there's little worth
in kindling a fire.
Some days a touch can be kind.

THE LONG HARVEST

When the stubble scrapes
and the corn, newly ripe,
scores weals across my hand
with its sting and its thin line of blood,
at least I shall never hear
a babe at my back, bawling in the bright sun
nor a child at my side, dragging on with his whine
of "Mother, I'm tired, Mother, I need to piss, Mother,
I need to go home, I'm hungry, Mother, I need to feed"

and I shall never feel
the ache at my hip or the small of my back,
or the sickness rise in my throat,
knowing I carry another bairn within.

In a bad year
I'll nurse my hunger alone. I'll never feel
the child grow sluggish and still
till it stiffens inside me.

The long harvest is shared,
but when winter comes
the cold is mine alone.

LOSS

The cold is mine alone
and the heat
and the time that day
when grey sky cleared to silver
and clouds raced across like hares.

And there was a lark –
and there are many larks, but on that day
I stood, heard and became
song, sky and lark

till I caught the lark in a song
but here is my loss:
the song entered the world
alone, and without my name.

LONGING

Not all husbands are bad.
Beatings come rarely to a good wife.
There may be praise, too, and a loving touch
at the birth of a boy
or a fine pottage, hot from the hearth.

VILLEIN

My lord would have put me to wife
with a sturdy ploughman
but the ploughman fled.

I would have mated his man
but his man was sent to the wars
where they hurt him. He did not return.

The children scream like crows
as they work on my lord's land.
They harrow me with their howls.

I am mocked like a bull at the baiting
but never pulled to earth,
never seized, never taken.

HYMN FOR ST. URSULA, TO BE SUNG ON HER DAY

Today, God's treasure house
is a vessel crammed with virgins.
You are standing at the helm.

O jubilate Deo
you bless God with your breath.
Your boat is balanced on blue

while the waves unfurl no monsters:
ten thousand virgins carol
within its wooden walls;

ten thousand seals are unbroken –
no scope for scorn or scolding,
no lure for Lenten lusts.

Soon the ungodly men
will arrive to make you martyrs;
so louder sing *Gaudete,*

be certain of God His mercy
and die *in Jesu Christi*
supported by His saints.

BÉGUINAGE

My father took me from the beguine house.
He made me a servant to my sister's son.

>	away from the women's voices
>	that scurry like mice after harvest –
>
>	away from the Lauds hymn
>	that soars like a lark in the heavens –
>
>	away from the slick rustle
>	of silk doing service to russet –
>
>	away from the ache of longing
>	for Christ and his lovely limbs –

My father took me from the beguine house.
He made me a servant to my sister's son.

ANCHORESS

Today, a glitter of gold,
blue, scarlet, bronze
spatters the stone wall
as women's voices – and girls' –
rise in the Matins song,
Te Deum laudamus,
and God responds from the bass,
sings back to the sunlight
where I walked once
when grass was wet
and my feet bare.

Today I take Christ's flesh
through the small hatch
and he melts, soft on my tongue,
to guard eyes and ears
from a scatter of birdsong
and light's lingering glance.

The saints and angels praise you.
Enrol me in their choir
and, when you come, Lord (soon
for the world needs judgment)
I shall be here to serve
and you will set me free
from this little room,
this little, little room.

PRAYERS REQUESTED OF AN ANCHORESS

that the harvest be good
that my crops thrive
that the yield of the black cow improve
that the brown cow bring forth a healthy heifer
that no witch overlook my pigs
that my son be not taken for a soldier
that the lord of the manor be blessed and his wife be blessed
                                          also
that I be not tempted to sloth
that the Lord forgive my sins and let me live with him in
                                          paradise
that my wife keep silence
that my husband be not diseased
that the rain come not in the day
that my daughter do her husband's bidding
that my daughter help with the harvest
that I bear strong sons
that my cottage be not swept away in the floods
that death, when it comes, be gentle
that I be not a beggar
that my husband be kind
that I survive childbed
that I be not with child
that the king's wars flourish
that there be a good peace in this land
that the children of the king's enemies fall ill
that the sky turn to black and the sun be darkened in the sky
that treason be prevented
that the heretics be found, condemned and burn for ever in the
                                          flames of Hell
that I come at last to God's loving mercy

THE WANTON

When I was young and wilful and would not wed
the blacksmith said he would have me to wife (and my father
willed it).
I denied him like a child
though I'd tasted twelve summers.
I had no wish for the flames of a stranger's hearth.
Besides, I feared the burnt arms of the blacksmith
that were blistered in the blaze.
I thought his form forged in the flames
and was wary of his warm weight.
So I strode single and reaped only for my father's house
and, when the breeze was bitter, sought my mother's kiss –
less hateful than a husband's hurting hands.

At harvest, I was strong and my cheeks burned.
I pulled the shift loose from my swelling breasts
and felt men's fingers reach for the rise of my breath
and I smiled. May God forgive me, I smiled
and did not look to see if any followed
the way I took.
So when he grasped me I was not surprised
nor when he held me still, pulled back the cloth
and pressed me down.
And whether I said yea or nay
I do not know
but I recall he cried out twice
as he planted a babe in my belly
and that he held me close
and kissed my brow
before he fled into the dew-soft dark,
and he said nothing.

Now from within the child reaches up to my throat.
It pokes at my skin, sends prickles into my flesh.
It punches my belly
out into shame, out into grief.
My knees ache from the stone flags of the church.
My fingers are shaped by the bead after bead I tell
evening beyond long day, day beyond waking night.

From church gate earth seems smooth, as water to swimming
                                                                           birds
but beneath my feet is the fierceness of ridged furrow.
I slip on sodden soil.
Air's ache assaults my arms.
The weight in my womb marks me wanton,
bears witness against me.

And when I come to the water
I shall not go in
for I testify against demons
who would drag me to self-slaughter.
I affirm self-slaughter is a sin
though the river is cool at my ankles
and the child within me dances, unafraid.

LA DAME À LA LICORNE

A girl, who is not quite real,
sits
in a field of flowers.

A unicorn,
who is not quite real,
canters toward her,
sprawls
and she does not move
as, with care,
he lays his great white head
beneath her girdle.

A finger reaches his face,
soundless –
she would not startle
a unicorn
whose dark eyes widen
and whose breath
is deep and slow.

EPITAPH FOR AN UNKNOWN PRINCESS
in the royal basilica of the abbey church of St Denis

The king my father loved me well
when I was young and not unknown.
Five years I flourished. Then, I fell.
The king my father loved me well
but no-one living now can tell
my name or face from faded stone.
The king my father loved me well
when I was young and not unknown.

ENCLOSURE

I – eviction

When we had heaved in the harvest
early against the rain –
and that year the rain came early –
then came the liveried men
from our lord on his liveried horses.
They said he was quit of our hands –
was quit of our quick, quick hands
that had stacked his corn into stooks –
that our backs had bent in his labour
this time for the last time
and now we must go like autumn.

We were amazed at the telling
for even the Norman yoke
merely numbered men and held them
and kept them safe in their place.
But this was a new thing –
a scatter of Satan's sowing
that bid us begone with nothing
or await the swing of the scythe.

Fathers fled first with their fondlings,
went quick before sky blackened.
They grabbed onto babies and bundles
and wandered away with their wives.
I stayed behind with the old folk.
Alone, I called on Christ's mercy

but God gave his gifts to the rich
who rose as rapid as ragwort.
He gave them my roof also
and set me loose on a road
when he welcomed the hedgers and ditchers
who carved up the land that was common.

II – lament

Sheep huddle at the ashes of my hearth.
I cannot card their wool, nor wash it.
Another woman winds it on her spindle.
I cannot see the weft and warp
nor the thread drawn into tightness across the loom.

III – plea

Time came I welcomed a hedge.
Then rain flattened the furrow.
I drank from the dirt of the ditch
and sheltered with creatures that scratch.

At priest's house I passed for a pilgrim
and held out my palm.
I shared the straw above stables
when monks offered shelter.

The soup I drank was thin, the bread green
and the ale sour.
I thanked God for his mercy
and heaped praise on all the givers.

So at last I came to locked gates
and there I stayed until sunrise,
being wary of the watch.
Then I entered the tall town

where I swear, I swear I stole nothing
though *an-hungered* and *a-thirst*,
and though I am a stranger
there was no-one to take me in.

I swear to you I'm no thief.
If you beat me as a beggar
I'll confirm that as your kindness
and then, if it be God's will,

let me go, to wander for ever
his world – so wide without walls.

VARIATIONS ON A HALF-REMEMBERED THEME

I

This is a tale. Once, in a land of ice
two children lived. They were twins. The boy
knew he would do great deeds. Meanwhile the girl
dreamed only that one day she'd become a mother.
And further off, in an icier land, a witch
allowed no change. The world froze in her mirror.

II

Another tale. A girl enters a mirror
to find herself in a different world of ice.
She takes her pack, sets out to conquer the witch
while at home there are tasks to be done. So the boy
sits and sews. His virtue pleases his mother
who praises him in these words: "just like a girl."

III

Another story. One day a robber-girl
climbs on a horse. They canter into the mirror
to steal its wealth. The robber-girl has no mother.
No-one has taught her to tremble or halt at the ice
or to pause for pity's sake. She passes the boy
who stumbles and slips. She leaves him as prey for the witch.

IV

The boy stumbles and falls. He is prey for the witch
and forgets his home, forgets his mother, the girl,
and knows only the witch's body, that he's a boy
and that something within him froze, a sliver of mirror
perhaps it was, or colder, a sliver of ice.
He calls the witch "my love" and sometimes "mother."

V

Mothers are made to mourn. Here is a mother
who knows she has lost two children to the witch
and she cannot grieve. Her heart, like the world, is ice
and the snow falls. She can find no grave for the girl
she once was, nor can she see in the mirror
anything real. There's no girl there, no boy.

VI

You want a conclusion? Happiness for the boy?
The twins restored at length to a grieving mother?
Imagine it then. The mother looks in the mirror,
two children emerge, she smiles as the witch
shrivels or melts. Elsewhere the robber-girl
canters away on her horse across the ice.

VII

But perhaps the boy in his heart still longs for the witch
as the mother prays for the days when she was a girl.
As for the mirror – it's there. Just look in the ice.

AFTER THE VALLEY WAS FLOODED

Having left, she learned again the shape of fields,
new names for birds, the way another town
clung to the hillside, then fanned out
running roads across slopes, drawing trains
from powerful cities. Marrying, she became fluent
in her new place, as rivers are
the same and not the same, altering their course.

There was a blue brooch once, lost for ever
on a careless morning. There were rocks,
children who climbed, and gulls that called.
There was a father's crumpling smile.
In her new world, the old shapes lost their force.
At night, she dreamed of distant bells. By day
the unused words twisted about her heart.

GELYNOS

(Night waits)
                Bats jitter
over
      hills as dark as moss

and the road may end
as here
      in the space
between three trees.
                    It's cool now
where desires were hot,
petitions urgent.

But here, a congregation
found its own power,
rose and then crumbled.

Slate fell, cracked into bracken.
Tombs were lapped in green.

AT ALNWICK CASTLE – AFTER THE WRECK OF THE FORFARSHIRE

After helping rescue survivors, Grace Darling, daughter of the Longstone lighthouse keeper, accepted an invitation to visit the Duke and Duchess of Northumberland.

'And there was no more sea.'

Inland tastes of chaff and honey.
The earth is rich with grain.
Pigs, sheep are humble. Silent, the soft-eyed calves
tender their docile necks to the farmer's knife
and streams run sweet.

By night the seals swim close
pushing through nightmare in a moment's grace
till they slide, laugh, clap – bloated mistakes
disturbing dreams.

The taste of salt is gone.
I am made soft as soil. My task is set:
obey the ladies, watch, give answer to their
endless questions.

*'Books and my father schooled me –
I learned the Bible, sermons, tales of peoples,
countries elsewhere.'* Read polish clean write cipher –
oceans and words.

*'Always busy at home,
we harvest the sea. Cormorant, sea-weed, eggs
are good for food.'* Seals we must skin and salt,
which we take, eat.

The woman flapped like a bird
when we rowed to Harcar. *'Spray was fierce, hit hard'*
at her closed and stone-dead sons whom we took, laid
limp on black rock.

'But surely suffering saves?'
Riches do not ennoble. I have been carried
far from my work and set among ladies –
dull, indolent, useless,
wicked as seals.

GRACE POOLE, 1847

In the great house, up on the dark moor,
fires are lit by invisible hands.
You might add, maybe a wife or two
is kept in the attic. But this is
far less than everyday misfortune.
Others, rising before birds shatter
night, must fetch water, serve in silence,
feed, mend, make, clean, tend – names few, face-less.

What surprise, then, should some fires escape
permitted bounds? . . . first, the master's bed,
bright with mute anger, then the great house
flames. And we shall get them yet, who own
our years, distant as the rich orphan,
one of them, remarrying her class.

MALVOLIO IN PRISON
"sometimes he is a kind of Puritan"

Slivers of light dissolve
to pin pricks, flicker out.
It is moss-dark, grass-dark,
stone-dark. My lady's care
trickles in laughter, fails.

Her world was a promise
lightly implied, lightly
forgotten in swift joys.
Her world was my order
and lightly set aside.

The sea knocks at my cell.
Its purifying weight
bears down on the nude shore
and the gulls flee to voice
cries of the forsaken.

I am one with the earth
torn by the rich to clothe
brief whims. Now I am sick,
naked and starved. I thirst –
you visited me not.

Light-bearing priest and fool
tempt with false proofs. My breath
halts, and my richest dreams
have slid away, melting
through darkness and black stone.

But God is in the dark.
I am his steward who
can raise the hidden soil
against its ravishers
and choke them with its wealth.

AT THE CHATEAU D'IF
an epilogue to an imagined play of The Count of Monte Cristo

and the moral of the tale?
Trust no-one. The good
will probably suffer. Pirates may be kind.
As for your friends –
how quickly they slide
into success. They left you behind.

Learn all you can.
Who knows what obscure custom
or what tongue, heavy in the mouth,
will help your disguise?
When this is done, you'll never
rest as yourself. The honest sailor
followed commands. He asked few questions
and was mostly loved.

Do your best to remember
that summer of swifts
– black flecks in the sky –
and the gulls that were shrieking
"Keep out. Keep out."
You observed, even then. The cicadas
fell quiet at your approach.

> The honest sailor
> went on his way.
> Where he has gone to
> none can say.

Though rulers change,
prisons persist.
One warder offers soft words,
another a kick.
Both have families.
Soon they'll be home
where it's easy to forget.

If you want vengeance
– what else is left? –
you know you'll have to pay.
Loyalty too has a price
which is best supported by threats.
One day luck may be yours.

The wedding feast
may be interrupted.
There's no going back.
You can tell the truth
as much as you want.
You won't be believed.

DRIVING TO THE MOON, WITH GHOSTS

I take the wheel
of the black jalopy
forgetting I can't drive.

Even at 70, it's a long trek.
I wait for air to thin

and the earth spins, showing
beachcombers, mudlarks,
oil aflame, forests,
milk-spun clouds
oozing a clear trickle.

But you're beside, behind me.
I feel safe. Gravity
lessens, oxygen slips away.
You don't need breath, and this past year
I've learnt to do without.

The way's smooth now, and clear. We're joking
about green cheese and men in the moon.
Someone quotes Wells, or Verne,
conjures a simile, a film
when it all starts to go wrong.

Behind me there's a gasp.
Hands ease. A mouth
fills up with blood.
Eyes close.
Beside me there's a toppling crash

and I'm driving alone
and tears can't fall
here, in this airless night

so I drive on (don't mock)
and on
to a hard stillness
where touch endures
like the first footfall
more than a thousand years.

AT COLDRUM STONES

In the sharp light
we paused for coffee.
The stones held their secret.

I asked nothing. We sat,
shared cake, were silent mostly
in the sharp light.

You knelt by the fence, let
a scene compose in your camera:
the stones with their secret

(which my mind caught
only as a blur
in the sharp light)

 and warm hills slanted to meet
 blue sky, leaves stilled by the shutter.
The stones held their secret.

Time didn't stop. You brought
something precise – a memory
to the sharp light.
The stones held their secret.

AFTER VERMEER

Notes spill
into unbreathed air.
Keys are unpressed. The bow
lies noiseless on the strings.

Please look away.
My silks
refuse to rustle.
Please   look away

DELFT, 1661

In 1654 Vermeer's home city of Delft was wrecked by the massive explosion of a gunpowder store. Vermeer's painting was made seven years later.

One half of it is sky. Dark clouds
do not descend, shadows
do not rise up but rest
water-logged, in a might-have-been
from another time.

Roofs, sturdy brickwork
must have been here for ever
but, if you will, draw near.
Over the river's shimmer
small smudges of people
are up against walls. They don't matter.

Black and unmoving, barges float. Rust
never begins and ageing never ends.
Two women talk
of little things
here in this afterward
of no before.

Be safe. Pause in the frame. Know that
nothing has ever happened
and, if we stay here, nothing will.

DAVID IN FLORENCE

Squinting into the sun, he takes a stone
and, as when guarding sheep, lets loose.
The giant's forehead reddens, skews, his face
falls into sand. Just so the muzzle of the lion
ate earth. Then silence ends. He stands, alone,

cut into marble, set in bronze, to tell
princes their weakness must prevail. And the city
gazes up at the naked thighs, feels pity
for newly-muscled flesh. His victory's a marvel,
so they say, a sign all shall be well.

AFTER A SELF-PORTRAIT BY MURILLO

You bought.
You bought.
                    I sold
the ragged boys whose grin
trickled unwilling gold
from purse to open palm

and virgin after virgin
whose ecstasy you bought
shored up your shallow fame
(and mine). This is my trade.

My hand lies on the frame.
My gaze is unafraid.
You bought. You bought. I sold.
I satisfy a need.

PALAIS DES BEAUX ARTS

A child becomes man
and steps out of a tomb.
The torturer holds to his rope.
A woman kneels with the dogs.
She unleashes ointment. Her hair sweeps the floor.
Now, move along please. These are
everyday things.
A man steps from a tomb.
There is nothing to startle.
A mother clutches her child.
These are everyday things.
A torturer –
Now, move along please,
there's nothing to see.
These are everyday things.
A child –
There is nothing to see
so please, move along, move along, move along.

AD MAJOREM DEI GLORIAM
When he entered the Jesuit order, Gerard Manley Hopkins is said to have burnt his poems.

His sleeves are black. They lie
against the grain of polished oak.
His hands are bare.

Inside his head
a halcyon flaunts
and phrases spring like firefolk
bright as a silvered disk
in a cobalt sky.

He will be still.

It's easy now
to strip each page from spine,
bend back
        the stiff, black card,
to loosen lines

for he'd go halt, lame, blind
into the kingdom –
lonely too
could he unhusk himself
by nature, simply
as a tree unleaves.

The flames fatten
              but the words
cling to his fingers.
              Crafted lines
are, like this sacrifice,
              rhythmic as sex.

Lithe paper flickers.
A page spirals to light.

He chokes in the dust
of acrid words.

OCCUPATION

Just as before, a café tune
tinkles familiar bitter-sweet
and falling note from roughened throat
causes accustomed tears to well
as though the darkness never fell
or talk could be (or thought) quite free.
What if there's slightly less to eat
or silence sometimes comes too soon?

Let art console the homesick heart:
some light-stilled town or kitchen scene
wins the stiff uniforms release
from what their slightest gestures mean.
Discernment sets them miles apart
from all the damaged streets they police.

PAINTING IN THE MIDI, 1942

Why would you want to step beyond the window
into dense colour – scarlet, lavender-blue
and the green of jungle? Though there is
      a brown path, it leads

nowhere, but simply is. The frame protects. Safe
here, watch as the storm draws up its clouds and makes
not darkness on earth but radiant thunder –
      a sharp pool of light.

Seen once, in Toledo. Now in my lush south,
France and not-France . . . here is constraint, compromise,
Art. Northward there's parched submission and terror
      routine as waking.

But now paint is the problem. Can I inspire –
with tone, shade, palette and diligent brushstroke –
a moment's rapture? Oh pause, feel my delight
      when a skylark sings.

AT THE *VÉL' D'HIV'*

and a girl flicks her fringe, and a finger
is black with ink. A boy

pulls down his jacket, another slicks the hair
back from his forehead. He reveals

two acne pits. On the track, a mother kneels
and with her hankie scrubs away at the stain

on a child's wet face. A cheek
crumples, a hand loses a coin,

a mouth gapes. A trickle of urine
snakes down a leg, like a drop of rain

or a tear. An old man creases his brow
to attend to his book. There's a frayed lace

and hands which fix and untie and fix
– but you don't want to see. Think of them

as parcels, lad, flocks if you must –
simplest to say they're "goods for conveyance."

Fill in the forms, be polite, be firm
(you're a smart lad) and do what you're told.

Eat well if you can. It won't be long. Look after
family first. Sleep soft. Quite soon you'll get

the trick of it.

THE FATE MOTIF
Garmisch – 1945

Those notes are everywhere. Spring brings defeat.
Even the lark sings doom.
The conqueror has music too. This is arrest.

        As the old man
descends the stairs, his voice
strengthens. He proclaims his worth.
His *Salomé*. His *Rosenkavalier*.

And what could he have done
about the disappearances, the camps?
He saved lives. He killed none.

He tells his music-loving captors
(who flattened opera-houses)
how shapes change

from death into delight,
skip out as flame
then mourn and fall.

If "no-one understands it rightly"
as Goethe says, what chance for him?
But he can write it now, for them.

Your oboe, corporal, will play my world
and breach the limits that you placed on me.

Finger the fate motif. Breathe out the dance.

BARBARIANS, AD 98

Writing the life of his father-in-law Agricola, Tacitus invented a speech for the Caledonian chieftain Calgacus.

The line where empire ends.

Pause. And the weighty Roman summer
bears on his back.
                His duty calls up
distance, rain and cold,
Rome at its boundaries, a war
beyond our gods, our roads, our circuses.

Beneath fresh herbs, the smell of rotting fruit
disturbs him. Blood, too, is somewhere in the street.
He wants his farm, country simplicity,
cool breezes. City food's too rich.
He's tired of silverware and coloured cloth.

This task detains him. At his call
a slave brings wine and olives, mops his brow.
He sips.
        He needs to know
words in a barbarous tongue, not shaped by Rome.

It comes to this:
A man, on a steep hill, faces death,
prepares to kill. Men are assembled,
weapons grasped. A speech is made.
He needs the words. They know what Rome is,
there, where earth ends.

                Pirates
of all the world ... He has it now –
their quaint, unmannered tongue.

This pillaging
they dignify as ordered government.
(Can he square that with the Emperor?
"I'm a historian. Besides, my duty …"
He'll write a preface; things are better now.)

Still the barbarian speaks. *They take a land*
and make a wilderness. They call it 'peace.'

WATCHING BIRDS IN TIME OF WAR

Tell me, augurer,
when gulls curve above concrete,
what do their wings spell?

Why do spindle-legged
starlings startle and vanish
before car's faint hum?

The morning air is
thick with frost. Weight it also
with hefty meaning.

TESTAMENT: IN AN EMBANKMENT GARDEN

Blackbird, I see this garden
        should have been planned for you

and now it's yours, as the woman
        sprawled on the bench spits phlegm

and the man clutching the railings
        taps at his phone, willing the screen to load

but there's no reply, and the sky brightens
        and doves descend, a bicycle crumples

and roots wrench roads out of true, a tree twists
        to demolish a wall, leaves break through brick –

so sing, blackbird. The river rises. We dying bequeath
        this garden to you and to your heirs

and ask that you use it well who stay
        – and look at me, blackbird, now and sing

till you splinter air with your sweetness –
        here, blackbird, here – let me hear you sing as I vanish

The Little Book of Illusions: scenes from a history of magic

TRANSFORMATION

I ask for rice, any rice, and I pour the grains
into the flask. I have it here
and look, you can see the rice
through the sides, which are glass.
There is nothing strange.
I shake the flask.
I cover it with a scarf.
I tap with my wand
and I shake again,
then stop. From the flask, I pour
for you coffee, for you wine.
Drink it – you see, it's good.
And I ask for thread,
discover a spider.
I put them both in the flask
and I say, "Spider, spin"
and gently I shake the flask
and cover it with my scarf,
and tap it with my wand
and I shake again
then uncover – the flask is filled
with scarves, with silken scarves.

I extend my hand, which is bare.
The palm is wide, the fingers
straighten and bend. See the quick flick,
and the twist of the wrist
as the fist forms
fast, without threat.
It opens to disclose
an egg, which I take, crack
into a glass bowl, where, in an instant

a hen sits, flutters her feathers, clucks
and discloses another egg. Soon there's a row
of hens on a perch. I place each hen in a bowl
where it clucks — and I crack each egg
disclosing the yolk and I bow. You applaud.

My breath pushes my lips
and I form "a bird." So perhaps you see
a seagull, perhaps a wren, or perhaps you hear
a phrase from a song by Strauss, or you glimpse
the glitter of gilded wings. Then I say
"It's a dove" and you see it, there, where it flutters
high on the rafter. It becomes
a flurry of white. I let it dissolve in air
to resolve, inkily black, an exquisite curve
of dark — till it's silent, fixed in its shape
as an echo only, a ghost or at best
a dead dove read and rotting
fading from sight and suddenly
empty. Nothing.
A blank, white page.

THE VANISHING PRINCESS

Night
and he calls her
every night
from dark
to a different place
where she peers
slow
through the black frame
but she cannot smell
wine garlic sweat breath
and can hardly
hear
the shouts,
merely does
what they require:
shimmers
her dollface,
waves
a porcelain hand,
looks out
but only at the given time
and almost smiles

but the black box
and the black earth
have a stronger call

so she fades
sweetly

knowing
she will be called
again
on another night
for another crowd
in another place.

INSTRUCTIONS FROM ROBERT-HOUDIN

When you furnish a room, choose as befits a gentleman: nothing cheap nor vulgar, no ostentation – all restrained, all refined. Let your craftsmen use the best fabrics, the most expensive materials and ensure they work with the utmost care. There must be no hint of tricks or a clever sham. Think of your audience; your backdrop is their life. Give them no chance to question or suspect; you are as good as they.

Avoid extravagance in dress. Find a good tailor who is well-acquainted with current styles. Adhere to the mode of the moment; to be in advance of fashion is as unseemly as adopting last year's mode. Slight understatement is the mark of modesty and elegance. Refrain at all costs from the swirling cloak or the wizard's pointed hat. Your shirt should be plain, your waistcoat unemphatic. A tail-coat is proper. Carry a top-hat and cane. Keep your hands gloved and see that the glove fits perfectly to each finger. Bare hands are unwise. You'll see them checking your palms, knuckles and nails. It's not your magic they suspect but your class. When you perform, remember you're one of them.

Tell them their thoughts. You know what they want. The urges that drive them drive you too. The slightest gesture, the faintest indrawn breath – you'll know what it means. Watch for the blush, the lowered eyelid. Listen. In the end you can read them blindfold. Do it. See? Always the same desire, the same image, the same wish to conceal and be known.

The orange tree comes next. Start with a pip. Take it from a real orange, which you should pare before them. Let them smell the fruit – taste it, if they will. All you need is a single pip. Plant it. As you raise your hand, the tree will follow. Watch. It unfurls leaves, it blossoms, it sprouts fruit. Butterflies flaunt unbidden. Let the watchers marvel – and note how little it takes to achieve their gasps.

Last, you must take your child – the one you love above all, for whom all this is done. Rest his arms upon poles. Talk to him. Then, when he's ready, let them smell the ether. They will see him succumb. Hush. Raise him gently in your arms. Trust that the air will be kind as you let him go, and take the poles away. Now watch him sleep. You could watch him sleep for ever. But you take him up again and set him down, you wake him, he rubs his eyes and the trick is done. The people cheer and pay and cheer as if they never saw a sleeping child before. Perhaps they never did.

You're done now. It's enough.

So you will find your way to fortune. Let them forget your fame. When you've earned enough you can retire. They'll forget you were ever a showman – if you're rich enough. You'll set your children free. They can be whatever you wish: gentlemen, officers. You can retire safely, knowing their future is assured.

ROBERT-HOUDIN EN ALGÉRIE

You are ruled by the sword. I come to set you free.
Listen. I come in peace. The Emperor sent me.
You know who that is? I tell you. The big king.
The big king does not want war. No war. *Comprenez?*

Look. My trunk is empty. Bring me your strongest man.
Tell him to lift. He's strong, he takes it in one hand
and lifts. He smiles. His muscles barely flex.
See how easy it is. Tell him to set it down.

Now I will make him weak, womanly weak.
I am raising my arm. I have French magic.
I use it only for good, peace against war.
Tell him to lift again. He can't. His strength is sick

but he won't give in. He can't. He's weaker
than a child. He howls. You can hear the muscles tear
but he doesn't stop. He sweats and heaves and strains
and it won't budge. Stop. This is how we conquer.

This is our magic. If you give us land,
no-one need die. The Emperor is kind.
You need not crawl like dogs. Accept our mercy.
Please, do what we say. I can see you understand.

THE AETHERIAL SUSPENSION
Eugène to Robert-Houdin, 1870

Father, I'm writing this
in love and duty, and I don't know where I am.
No matter now. The battle's done
and I was brave, I think. At least
I didn't run. None of us ran.

Father, I am not writing this,
I can't. But once I learned – do you recall? –
to catch loose thoughts from air,
to read a woman's eyelash' quiver
and scrawl a strand of scent
loose on white card. You'd blindfold me
to pluck an embryo thought
still raw, out of the back
of a man's head. Father,
you taught me this. Do you remember?

Father, I'm sending this
across torn fields, smashed villages,
through angry armies to the city where
you starve, they say. Unpick the words.

I cannot see the wound.
They tell me that it's bad
and there's no ether here.
I smell the orange that you split.
You spun the pip,
burst it to flower and fruit.
Butterflies here,
real as the ones you made,
are red and buzz like flies.

You raised my arms, laid them on poles,
muffled my face.
The ether came –
I hurt. I want to drink.
You held me up and laid me on the air.
You took the poles away.

Lay me on air now, Father.
Lay me on air.
Fill up the air with blooms
and fruit, and wings –
then gently, let me go.

SHARPER

It's a joke, surely?
>but the follow-spot
has got you in a glare

harsh as the carpet's soft.
>There's a stink of lime. The boards
creak at your sudden weight.

and it's *Hearts, diamonds, spades,*
>*clubs*. Breathe in. How heavily
you pause, take in the cards,

rough-knuckled hands which splay
>a deck: holding it
first as a fan then up to a tower

tumbling, as *Club, diamond, heart,*
>*spade* – "Take a card. Any card."
And you pick, pause, look. The eight

of spades. The eight of spades.
>So black leaves hover
in air (there are eight) and they hold

a place in your mind, but beware.
>The quick hands shuffle: it's *Heart,*
diamond, club, spade. "Another" –

so it begins again. Hot sweat
>gleams on his brow. "Pick a card."
You reach. Take slowly. Turn and inspect

the two of clubs. You have heard
>that in wars – in the hush a cry:
two men with clubs drag a child –

till the scene etches its way
        fast to your brain. You won't forget
but he tells you still, "Remember."

He's smiling now. The cards lie flat
        before his empty hands.
"Pick again." Without thought

your hand reaches, it selects a card,
        and without thought you have to
look. It's a jack-the-lad,

it's a careless, one-eyed boy –
        think love, the jack of hearts –
guileless in a world of number,

of rules, of fortunes lost
        and fortunes gained.
It's heart and jack. Now list

all three: eight spades,
        two clubs, and the picture
whirls, is gone as he spreads

his hand – but you must remember
        Clubs, diamonds, spades, hearts.
There's that other one, the one-eyed boy

who falls, childish – but the cards tilt,
        sway, and it's *Spades, diamonds,*
clubs, hearts and he says "Which one was first?"

holding out, face downward,
        a single card. As you say
"the eight of spades"

(and you see eight leaves in air)
        he turns the card and it's right
before you. There's a smile, a bow,

applause. "So which came next?"
>His fingers have grasped
a card. A war twists

through your brain, a child dead –
>and "it's clubs," you say, "the two"
and it's there on the board.

Then he reaches behind your ear
>and you touch the card as he holds it
still. You think of the one-eyed boy

and he says, "Now tell me – the last –
>what was it – the third card?"
Spades, clubs, diamonds, hearts.

This time you'll win. And you say "diamonds,
>the queen." He turns the card. And there
she lies: unsmiling, regal, double-eyed.

RESTORATION

                Loss is neat
          and precise as the tock
        of your grandfather's watch
     which a hand unclasps, holds out
for the man in the black frock-coat
            whose sympathy
          is a stern, slow smile:
    "I do what I like – you don't mind?"

  You bow your head as the golden
     gleam is draped, tight-knotted
      in a red, white-spotted cloth

  and he lifts the hammer, lets fall
         and unwraps

springs coils wheels motion balance

    scatter
        there's a smashed face

                    numbers are gone

    time stopped.

Stopped time

gone are numbers

smashed face, there's a
scatter

wheels coils springs balance motion

unwraps and
he lets fall, and the hammer lifts.

In a white, red-spotted cloth
knotted tight, the golden
gleam is draped, as you bow your head.

"You don't mind I – like what I do?"
is a slow, stern smile
of sympathy -
for the man in the black frock-coat
holds out a hand which unclasps
your grandfather's watch
whose tock is precise
and neat as loss.

UNSUNDERED

The piccolo squeals. Yes, Captain,
her lips are scarlet as I said.
Her skin? You can watch it whiten.

The saw carves its way. Bows scrape,
drag across catgut, the drum
has yet to roll. From your plush seat

you observe the taut criss-cross
– fishnet at knee, imagine
the white wrist and a pulse

suddenly fast, then halt
as her mouth opens wide to an O
that could mean surprise or delight.

Last year you learned
deafness. Today you trace
a single tear or a dot of sweat

snailing its course from eye to ear
and note with a shock
of distaste: she's not young,

her hair's fool's gold, and her neck
crinkles and sags.
But she'll do, she's afraid, and the saw

scrapes with a clarinet's rasp –
and beneath the box, surely, the first
drip of blood. Drumroll. She'll do

for the moment – and now her eyes stretch,
her feet twitch, and the light,
which sleeks her white face into mask,

has peeled back the flesh, and you think
of skulls, of the fingers' clench
at a rat-fur touch — but you're here

and the cut's sword-clean, and the air
thick with cologne. Drums. And the box divides.
Blood. As her eyes stare and her feet are still

till magic returns with the violins,
the halves of the box slide back, and the lid
rises. The hand that sawed is gentle

now, and gloved. Its reach
opens the box and a girl,
who is young again, steps out,

long-legged, a-glitter,
fresh with the rebirth sheen
you never chose.

But you can never say
which dead stay dead, and which
are fitted back

to take the conjurer's hand
and stand smiling,
returned, remade.

THE PRIVATE BURYING GROUND OF BLACK HERMAN

It's not what we intended – but I'll swear
   it's what he'd have wanted.
Roll up, folks. Black Herman's dead.
Yup, you can lift his eyelid

and thumb his eye. You boy, there! – On your way
   or pay up. A quarter.
You'll see how the eyeballs stare.
Prick him? Sure – the pin's extra.

Boy and man I've been with him, since the time
   he travelled in medicine
summoning souls, and they came
sick and fretting for freedom

which is in poor supply down south – but please, Sir,
   don't you concern yourself;
you don't hail from hereabout …
A dollar unlocks my mouth.

They were filled with fancy tales, so he'd claim
   he came from the jungle –
a Zulu, who'd taken sail
to conjure mounds of cornmeal

and raise rabbits for the pot. They cheered as
   he shucked off the grief knots,
slipped the rope and stood upright
frightening folk into fits

– white folk, that is, for he told us: his people
   had slipped from the slavers
freed as foretold by Moses –
Well, he'd talk their wallets loose

though folk do nothing for free – they all charge,
   each preacher, carpenter,
tailor. We'd reckon each tear
in the tent at a dollar

and calculate Jim Crow miles, all the print
   on banner and playbill.
The poor pay cash on the nail;
they get no gain from goodwill –

but you, Sir, you won your wealth. Folk like you
   can afford their good faith –
when every man's for himself
and there's gold from a good death.

No coffin held such a corpse as Herman.
   Everyone knew he was
(save Christ) best in the business,
dying in public to rise,

dimes still on eyes, from the soil. Above, we
   shifted earth, we shovelled –
tough work in a time of toil –
so dirt on a dead face fell

again and again, and he never flinched
   for what was left to fear?
He was, as he said to me,
many times dead already.

His life was leased like the dust when we pitched
   where the soil was thinnest;
stones were the only harvest,
dry earth was brittle as rust,

the clay cracked, the lean kine lowed – they devoured
   acres, days – and children
cried for some food or a sign –
So we sold RESURRECTION:

poor folk can rise if they choose, after death
   or before, like Jesus –
only trust! and none can hold us.
Ours is all power that is.

So we took their trust and transformed drab lives,
   robbed them of fear, left them
hopeful, courageous, reborn –
and if it was a trick, what then?

It wasn't the worst. Sure, they paid with dimes
   needed for decent food,
perhaps they couldn't afford
to be brave or free from dread

but soon as he rose and dust fell away
   from his flesh, they found that
his strength conquered all folk feared:
hunger, hatred – and the rest

that's best not said, till the day he stumbled
   on stage and turned halfway
to a trick, his face still grey
as dust, and his eyes empty.

His fingers reached for his head, then his heart
   as he stopped short, toppled,
lay lengthwise – "Huzzah," folk howled.
Thinking it a trick, they cheered

then hush, hush – I heard his breath rattle, and,
   at once, nothing. Sayeth
God, through John: *The wind bloweth
where it list, and goes, like death,*

to some place else, and where, no-one can tell.
   Well, he's gone, Black Herman
and we head north. The show's done.
We'll give him back to the ground

We'll have hymns, preaching, prayers – then, it's my time
    to tour as a Herman –
small tricks to start: a potion,
the something-for-nothing turn

that starts with an empty hat or a bag
    that's brimful of rabbits:
hope parcelled out in tid-bits.
My ware's wonder, as he taught:

On stage, startle them! Be flash – for at last
    all voices will vanish,
pain, so they say, will perish.
Grieve quietly – and grab the cash.

BESS, 1936

Seeing I had the knack
of being small, he taught me
to be invisible: to vanish
into a sack shut in a closet
till he cut me free.

I used to dance. One day
he took me to a wood,
blew on my arm and when I saw
my father's name in ash –
well pardon me, I won't divulge the trick.

I followed him
and times were hard and places too.
My folks said never to come back.
I didn't. Soon I was on a stage
in a bright light and spoke
words from the dead which he'd explain

meaning that they should not be fooled
as he was not, that there were phonies
out there looking for a quick buck
who never knew his father called him "Ehrich"
or that his mother had no English.

He'd always check in with the police,
ask them to lock him up and then break out.
He was chained everywhere. When they threw him
off cliffs, in rivers – every time
he'd come back gasping to the same applause.

No gun nor bomb could touch him.
He'd catch bullets in his hand.
Almost, you'd think, he'd beaten the big D
till the final punch
ripped into pain and stilled him.

"I'm a fake," he said. Well I knew that.
Why would I want him different than he was?
Once he was gone I carried on
best as I could and waited all the time.

He never whispered "Rosebelle" in my ear –
or if he did I never heard.
I'm growing deaf. Besides, it's been ten years
and that's enough to wait for any man
living or dead. I'll put the candle out
for the last time. There's no afterwards.

When I'm gone, bury me with his bones.

AT THE STATION OF MONTPARNASSE

Welcome to the café of the future.
        Here is the station of Montparnasse.
The park is closed. They are clearing the square
        for old men who stand with medals and banners.

Here is the station of Montparnasse.
        I am your entertainment for today.
The old men who stand with medals and banners
        will not disturb you. Watch, for your pleasure –

I am your entertainment for today.
        I have here a sheet, white as a page.
I will not disturb you. Watch, for your pleasure.
        This is your history, could you rewrite it.

I have here a sheet, white as a page.
        First you must take your time and look your fill.
This is your history, could you rewrite it.
        The star-child weeps for his stolen tomorrow.

Now you must take your time and look your fill:
        the beggar extends her creased brown palm;
the star-child weeps for his stolen tomorrow;
        the workman fixes the cardboard of his home.

The beggar extends her creased brown palm –
        Give nothing. Watch, I am raising the sheet.
The workman fixes the cardboard of his home.
        It has nothing to do with you. You are here for the
                                        show.

Give nothing. Watch. I am raising the sheet.
        The streets are silent. Insistent voices
have nothing to do with you. You are here for the show.
        I twitch the sheet once, twice, three times.

The streets are silent. Insistent voices
        fade into whiteness. Past and present are empty.
I twitch the sheet once, twice, three times,
        and let it fall. The station of Montparnasse

fades into whiteness. Past and present are empty.
        The men in medals are gone. No star-child,
                          beggar or workman.
Let them fall. The station of Montparnasse is nothing.
        I will not trouble you any longer.

The men in medals are gone. No star-child, beggar or
                                  workman.
        The park is closed. They are clearing the square
and nothing will trouble you any longer.
        Welcome to the Café of the Future.